D1521274

LIFE IN THE FAST LANE

INSIDE A SPEEDBOAT

COLLIN MACARTHUR

Cavendish Square
New York

Published in 2015 by Cavendish Square Publishing, LLC
243 5th Avenue, Suite 136, New York, NY 10016

Copyright © 2015 by Cavendish Square Publishing, LLC

First Edition

Website: cavendishsq.com

This publication represents the opinions and views of the author based on his or her personal
experience, knowledge, and research. The information in this book serves as a general guide
only. The author and publisher have used their best efforts in preparing this book and disclaim
liability rising directly or indirectly from the use and application of this book.

CPSIA Compliance Information: Batch #WS14CSQ

All websites were available and accurate when this book was sent to press.

Library of Congress Cataloging-in-Publication Data
MacArthur, Collin.
Inside a speedboat / by Collin MacArthur.
p. cm. — (Life in the fast lane)
Includes index.
ISBN 978-1-62713-037-0 (hardcover) ISBN 978-1-62713-039-4 (ebook)
1. Motorboat racing — Juvenile literature. 2. Motorboats — Juvenile literature. I. Title.
GV835.M33 2015
797.12—d23

Editorial Director: Dean Miller
Art Director: Jeffrey Talbot
Production Manager: Jennifer Ryder-Talbot
Production Editor: David McNamara

Packaged for Cavendish Square Publishing, LLC by BlueAppleWorks Inc.
Managing Editor: Melissa McClellan
Designer: Tibor Choleva
Photo Research: Joshua Avramson, Melissa McClellan
Copy Editor: Catherine Collison, Janis Campbell

The photographs in this book are used by permission and through the courtesy of: Cover photo, AP Photo/Jerry
S. Mendoza; p. 4 © Jurijs Novikovs/Dreamstime.com; p. 6, 22–23 © Chuck Wagner/Shutterstock.com; p. 9 Vira
Mylyan-Monastyrska/Shutterstock.com; p. 10–11, 32–33, 35, 39 © Darren Brode/Shutterstock.com;
p. 12 © 3777190317/Shutterstock.com; p. 15 Pedro Monteiro/Shutterstock.com; p. 16–17 © Rui Ferreira/
Shutterstock.com; p. 18, 30 © Darren Brode/Shutterstock.com; p. 20 © Gabriella Ciliberti/Shutterstock.com;
p. 25 © Neacsu Razvan Chirnoaga/Dreamstime.com; p. 27 © Christopher Halloran/Shutterstock.com;
p. 28 © Anatoliy Lukich/Shutterstock.com; p. 36 © i4lcocl2/Shutterstock.com;
p. 40 © Steve98107/Dreamstime.com

Printed in the United States of America

CONTENTS

INTRODUCTION 5

1 FIERCE AND FUN 7

2 AUTO-MOTOR
MARVELS 13

3 A NEED FOR SPEED 21

4 SUPER AND SWIFT 29

5 REVVED UP
FOR RACING 37

WORDS TO KNOW 42

FURTHER READING 44

RESOURCES 45

INDEX 47

Racing a speedboat is challenging and exciting.

INTRODUCTION

Words can hardly capture all the sounds of racing as the roar of the engine makes a deafening noise along the water when powerboat racing begins. It reminds you of a racetrack, but instead of pavement, powerboat races take place on rivers, lakes, and ocean waters. As soon as engines were used to power boats, a new, fast, and exciting sport was invented.

Today, men and women race boats that have huge engines. Some of these engines have the pulling power of a thousand horses. High-speed boats travel as fast as 220 miles (354 km) per hour. Racing on the water, however, is not just about speed. These boats must race around a track, just the way cars do in auto racing. Floating markers called **buoys** mark the racetrack. The boats move up to the starting line. A light flashes to start the race. The roar of powerful engines blasts across the shores. Sprays of water shoot up and the racers are off!

Offshore boat races are patrolled by helicopters.

Powerboats of all sizes are used in races. Smaller boats, up to 9 feet (2.7 m) in length, can move as fast as 95 miles per hour (153 km/hr). Larger boats race in offshore races, or races on ocean waters. These boats are usually much bigger, as long as 48 feet (14.6 m). They are also faster, traveling up to 150 miles per hour (241.4 km/hr). Sometimes these boats have two or three engines. Offshore powerboats can be expensive, with price tags up to several hundred thousand dollars.

A Powerful Club

Any two people who have boats can race down a river. But to be crowned a champion, you must belong to a racing group. The American Power Boat Association (APBA) sanctions and schedules races across the U.S. There are sixteen different **regions** of APBA racing. On any weekend, there are hundreds of races run in many different states. The APBA works with the Canadian Boating Federation so that racers from both countries can easily compete in either nation.

The Racing Dozen

The APBA has twelve **categories** of power-boat racing. The categories have to do with boat types and engine sizes. Some boats have inboard engines. Inboard engines are placed inside boats and beneath a cover. Inboard engines can be near the center or back of the boat. A metal bar called a **shaft** connects the engine to the propeller. The propeller spins around and pushes the boat across the water.

Other boats have outboard engines. Outboard engines sit on the back of the boat. The bottom part of the engine holds the propeller. The propeller sits in the water.

A Class Act

Within each category of boat racing, there is also a class, or type, of boat or motor. Some classes of racing boats are determined by the size of the motor used in the boat. The

Outboard engines are attached to the back end of speedboats.

Hydroplanes skim across the water's surface on a cushion of air.

hull (boat body) and the engine size determine other classes. Powerboats can have V-hulls, flatbottom hulls, twin hulls (**catamarans**), and **hydroplanes**.

Of course, there are too many categories and classes of powerboats to cover in this powerboating primer. Instead, we focus on some of the more popular types of powerboats and racing events that the APBA sanctions. After you finish reading, you'll want to do more of your own research.

FAST FACTS

The twelve racing categories of the
APBA have every kind of powerboat
you can imagine:

- Inboard
- J Class
- Offshore
- Outboard Drag
- R/C Model
- Events
- Inboard Endurance
- Modified
- OPC
- Pro
- Stock
- Unlimited

For an explanation of each category, check
out the APBA website at: www.apba.org

The F1 powerboats belong to the highest class of inshore powerboat racing. F1 boat races are similar to Formula 1 car racing.

C ars and powerboats have more in common than you might think. Inboard powerboat engines are modified versions of automobile engines. The size of the engine and the style of hull determine the racing class, and there are fourteen different inboard powerboat racing classes. The high-speed hydroplane class powerboats have engines that are 500 cubic inches (.008 m^3). The flat–bottom runabout class boats use a flat bottom and a small engine.

Speedy and Sharp

Runabouts come in different lengths, but the minimum length is 9 feet (2.7 m). They travel at speeds from 80 miles (129 km) per hour to more than 140 miles (225 km) per hour. Runabouts are very stable on the water. This class of racing allows boats to race side by side, making for an exciting race.

13

Engine Power

Runabouts race using different engine sizes. The class of a runabout is determined by its engine size. The engines range from 7.5 cubic inches (123 cm^3) to 69 cubic inches (.001 m^3). The larger the engine, the faster the boat. Also, the larger the engine, the longer the boat.

The winning edge goes to the racer with the best driving ability, when everything else is equal. Powerboat–racing drivers know their engines and their boats. They know when to run an engine at maximum speed. They also know when to slow down for a turn. Winning a race is often the result of how a driver runs the engine.

FAST FACTS

The total area of all the engine cylinders determines an engine's size. This is an engine's **displacement**. Engine displacement is measured in cubic inches or cubic centimeters. An engine displacement of 125 cubic centimeters has 7.6 in^3 of total area within the cylinders. The larger the displacement, the faster the boat.

The controls in powerboats are like those in cars—accelerator pedal, steering wheel, and rear-view mirrors—with one exception, no brakes!

Hull Shape Is Key

Runabouts have a flat bottom. The boat sits on two long hulls about 6 feet (1.8 m) apart. The hulls rest in the water and keep most of the boat out of the water. Only a few inches of the hull and the engine propeller sit in the water.

Air passes below the boat, but not enough to lift the boat off the water. A runabout is specially designed for high-speed turns.

Flatbottom runabout powerboats race around a buoyed track. Some races are three laps around a one-mile course. Other races are four laps around a three-quarter-mile course.

INSIDE A SPEEDBOAT

Runabouts are known for their long lean shape.

High-flying Hydroplanes

Hydroplane boats are specially designed to sit atop two curved hulls. These hulls sit higher in the water than the runabouts. Hydroplane hull designs allow air to flow under the boat. This trapped air lifts the boat so that it runs just above the water's surface at top speed. Sometimes the only part of the boat touching the water is the propeller, which makes these races especially magical.

Engineered for Boats

Hydroplane powerboats fall into classes depending on their engine size. Inboard hydroplane boats use gasoline-powered

All hydroplane boat drivers are required to wear a racing helmet and a lifejacket.

automobile engines. These engines are modified for use in a boat. Some of the popular car engines used in hydroplane boats are Ford, Plymouth, and BMW. Engine sizes range from 246 cubic inches (.004 m³) to much larger sizes. Inboard Hydroplane boat speeds range from 105 to 170 miles (169 to 274 km) per hour.

Cool Drivers, Hot Hydroplanes

Driving a boat in a group that is racing around a track at 130 miles (209 km) per hour is tricky. The spray that other boats give off during a turn can hit like a sudden rainstorm.

Still more dangerous is the hydroplaning action of the boats during a race. The cushion of air that the boats ride on can make driving difficult. If there's too much air, the boat could rise into the air and flip. But if there's suddenly no air beneath the boat, the nose can dive into the water.

Hydroplane races usually run two **heats** (elimination rounds) of three laps each. The hydroplanes run counterclockwise around a buoyed track. The driver uses a side fin to turn the boat in a level position. Hydroplane powerboats run well and fast on smooth water. If there are calm winds, the water is smooth. When it's windy, the water gets choppy. This makes hydroplane racing rough and dangerous. At high speeds, choppy water kicks the front of the boat into the air. If the front end gets too high, the boat will flip backwards.

Racers know how to handle their boats, understanding that their speed and the condition of the track can affect performance. Racers avoid damage and have the skills to steer their boats as safely as possible. Race officials often cancel a race when weather conditions are too dangerous.

Offshore racing boats are big and powerful.

A NEED FOR SPEED

Ocean racing has a glamour all its own. Whether it's the Persian Gulf in the Middle East, or off the Australian shores, this is an elite sport. These races are usually regulated by the Union Internationale Motonautique, the international governing body of powerboating.

Offshore Mammoths

You could call offshore boats the big daddies of powerboat racing. Offshore boat lengths range from 24 to 48 feet (7.3 to 14.6 m). They must be big because they race on the ocean. During a race, ocean waves and swells can be 6 to 10 feet (1.8 to 3 m) high. A small, nine-foot, runabout traveling at 120 miles (193 km) per hour could flip. A hydroplane powerboat might dive into a wave.

V-Hulls and Catamarans

There are two types of offshore powerboat hulls: V and twin (catamaran). The V-hulls

Big trucks haul offshore boats to race locations.

are wide above water and sharply pointed below water. This gives them their "V" shape. Catamaran hulls have two narrow V-hulls that allow air to pass below the boat. Some racers say V-boats handle better on ocean waters. Other racers say catamarans are faster. It all depends on which racing team you ask.

Inboard or Outboard?

Offshore boats have either inboard or outboard engines. Some offshore boats have

one engine, although others may have two or three engines. The number of engines, the size of the engines, and the size of the boats determine each class of offshore racing. There are more than fourteen different offshore racing classes. Engine sizes range from 375 cubic inches (.006 m^3) to more than 1,400 cubic inches (.023 m^3). Offshore boats can reach speeds of 150 miles (241.5 km) per hour. These boats can launch off ocean waves and get airborne—engine and all.

A boat's hull is made of fiberglass. Fiberglass is made from thin glass and plastic fibers. The fibers are pressed together to make a strong bond. Fiberglass is the best material for boat hulls because it is lightweight, flexible, and very strong.

Two for Two

Offshore powerboat races are long. They sometimes last for almost two hours and cover more than 160 miles (257.5 km) of ocean. The boats race around a series of buoys. Offshore boats have two crew-members. One person controls the speed; the other person pilots (steers) the boat. Offshore races require speed, driving skill, and endurance.

Drag Racing on Water

You've probably seen drag races in the movies or on television. Drivers speed down a stretch of road. In official courses, they line up and race down a quarter-mile (0.4 km) track to the finish line. Did you know there are drag races for boats, too?

It takes two people to run a boat in offshore races.

Drag-Racing Classes

The APBA has twelve classes of outboard drag racing. Four of these classes allow everyday boaters to race their boats. As long as two boats are of equal length and engine size, they can enter a race. These four drag-race classes make up the entry-level sportsman classes.

All four sportsman classes use production boats, or boats bought from a showroom dealer. These boats are the same as those you see on any lake or river. Some people use them for fishing or water-skiing. But sometimes, they take them to the races. The difference between the showroom boat and a drag-racing boat is in the engine. The drag-racing boat's engine is modified to make it more powerful. The more powerful a boat's engine is, the faster the boat can pick up speed. Getting the boat up to top speed quickly is the difference between winning and losing a drag race.

The way the engine is modified determines the class in which the boat is placed. More engine changes mean a higher racing class. Some racing classes only allow engine

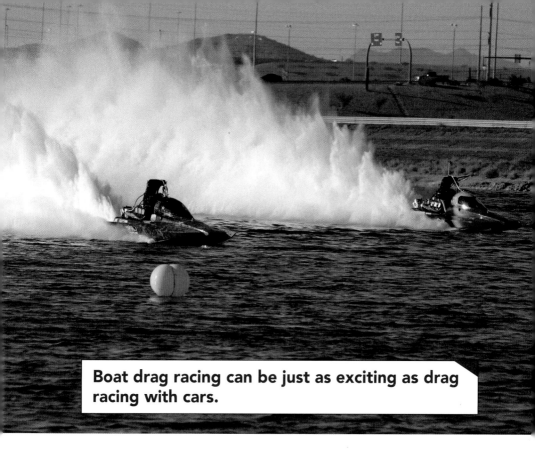

Boat drag racing can be just as exciting as drag racing with cars.

changes that are made using parts that you can buy at the local auto parts store.

The rest of the drag-racing classes are strictly for the professionals. These competitors use powerful boats, equipped with 300 **horsepower**, high-tech engines. While the hulls are similar to showroom boats, the souped-up engines can reach a speed of 100 miles per hour (161 km/hr) on a quarter-mile (.4 km) track. The speed of these specialty boats leads to some amazing races and exciting finishes on rivers and lakes.

Unlimited hydroplanes are the fastest speedboats.

The most popular speedboats today are also the fastest, the unlimited hydroplanes. These speed demons are a colorful blur on the water, and their sleek design and jet engines might make you think of rockets.

Jet Boat Racing

All hydroplane boats travel just above the water at top speed. Fans are familiar with the classic hydroplane's wake, or **roostertail**, rising high above the water. But unlimited hydroplanes use turbine jet engines to power them. When hydroplaning, often no part of the boat touches the water. The boat actually flies just above the water. The unlimited turbine jet engine can drive the boat 220 miles (354 km) per hour!

Danger exists all around at such high speeds. Winds can force the boat to flip. Waves and jet wash (the rush of wind made

Crew members and technicians make sure that the boat's engine is fine-tuned for the race.

by another boat's jet engine) also can cause flips. Boats can crash together while racing. Also, drivers can lose control of their boats.

Power for the Pilot

The unlimited's jet engine is sealed in a compartment behind the pilot. A jet engine is a turbine engine. A turbine is a fan that spins at high speed. The fan pulls air from the front of the engine and pushes it out the back to give the boat power. The higher the turbine speed, the more power and speed for the boat. During a race, unlimited hydroplane boats can average lap speeds of more than 160 miles (257.5 km) per hour.

High-Tech Safety

Unlimited hydroplanes must be designed carefully to protect both the pilots and the boats. Unlimiteds are designed using computers.

This high-tech designing makes them more **aerodynamic**, which means they can move through air more easily. A more aerodynamic boat is safer at higher speeds. The boat acts like a wing as it knifes through the air. If the boat is in the correct position, it stays in place. If the boat is out of position, it becomes dangerous for the driver and other racers. That is why an unlimited has two wings on the back of the boat. These are tail wings that stand at an angle. They steer the boat around the racecourse. The wings also help to keep the boat steady as it flies across the water.

Unlimited hydroplanes are made of fiberglass. They are longer, wider, and heavier than the inboard hydroplane boats. Unlimiteds have to be larger to carry their

Drivers who race boats with an enclosed cockpit are required to pass APBA certification.

jet engines safely. Unlimited hydroplanes are nearly 20 feet (6 m) long and 8 feet (2.5 m) wide. They sit low on the water. This low profile allows the boat to make tighter turns at higher speeds without danger of flipping.

Fighter Jet Cockpit

The pilot of an unlimited hydroplane sits in a sealed space called the cockpit. The cockpit is a lot like a jet–fighter cockpit. It is small and cramped. The cockpit has a steering wheel and a throttle to adjust the

speed. It also has dials that tell the pilot how the engine is performing.

The windshield dome that shields the pilot is made of a special plastic. This is the same plastic that is used for jet–fighter cockpits. It cannot shatter if an object strikes it. The dome protects the pilot from the rush of air that hits the boat at top speed. If the boat crashes, the pilot is safe from danger. Pilots wear jumpsuits that help them float in the water. They also wear crash helmets to protect their heads. There is constant revision of rules to make the races as safe as possible. For example, cameras are no longer attached to helmets because they have proved too heavy and dangerous in the event of a crash. Pilots also wear special protective body suits.

Traffic Jam on Water

Unlimited powerboat racing pilots are top professionals. They understand the excitement and danger of racing. Of course, all racers want to protect themselves as well as their boats. As many as twenty-four boats compete in a race. This is a lot of traffic for boats with no brakes.

Every competition has rescue teams ready to act in case there's a crash in a race. The team's quick response time saves pilots from harm and gets them to shore.

FAST FACTS

The Gold Cup Race on the Detroit River between Windsor, Ontario, and Detroit, Michigan, is the granddaddy of boat races. It has the oldest trophy of any motorsport.

An unlimited hydroplane pilot wearing a special protective body suit is entering the cockpit of the boat as a race on the Detroit River is about to start.

Boat races are popular all over the world. This young driver is practicing for the United Kingdom Juniors Powerboat Championship race.

There are junior racing classes and **circuits** that allow racers as young as nine years old to start. The APBA lists a junior racing schedule on its website.

But for now, while you're still a fan, you can take your pick of races to see across the country. Races take place in every state. In North America, Canada has a long racing tradition. The APBA and Canadian Boating Federation work together to make races easily accessible to the neighboring nations. There are also international race circuits. Powerboat racing has categories and classes for every fan around the world. In Europe, where powerboat racing is a big tradition, the sport continues to be popular. Another growth area is in the Middle East, where the sport is attracting an international crowd. Of course, powerboat racing also has fans in countries such as Australia, a sports-loving nation that is surrounded by water.

In the U.S., each racing category has different regional races. The outboard drag–racing circuit has sixteen regions around the country. A region can be made up of two, three, or four different states. During a racing season, racers gain points that help them get to other competitions. Late in the season, regional champions race against each other in national races. The winners of the national races become the national champions of a class.

Fun for Fans

Race day is exciting because fans have many chances to see races from beaches

FAST FACTS

According to the APBA, junior hydroplanes and runabouts (40 mph) welcome racers as young as nine years old. These are the types of boats for ages nine to twelve. AX hydroplanes and runabouts (50 mph) are for ages twelve and up. All junior racers must wear official safety gear, including a helmet, a lifejacket, and Kevlar sleeves and pants. The Kevlar material—used for all racers—helps protect the racer's body.

Going to powerboat races can be a fun and exciting way to spend a day with your family.

to riverbanks. The APBA has race locations and dates listed on its website. Local newspapers cover the bigger races.

A day of powerboat races is a day of celebration. As a warm-weather sport on the water, racing offers plenty to see and do. There are often food tents, music, and vendors selling souvenirs as fans arrive early and make a full day of it. There are also areas for fans to see the powerful boats up close and admire the designs of the boats. Boat manufacturers are usually present on race days. Most of these boat makers also sell family boats. They display

Classic Gar Wood triple–cockpit wooden runabout at Lake Tahoe in California.

their watercrafts so that fans can look at the boats closely.

Fans have many places on the shore from which to watch the racing. Racecourses measure from 1 to 2 miles (1.6 to 3.2 km) around a track. The track is laid out with brightly colored buoys.

Fantastic Fun

Being a fan of powerboat racing is all about having fun. Before and after the races, many powerboat pilots meet with their fans.

FAST FACTS

The name Gar Wood is legendary for speedboat buffs.

The Detroit-area inventor and entrepreneur not only invented and built boats, he raced them. Five times he ended up breaking the world record in water speed. Besides racing on the Detroit River, he also raced on the open water with his "Miss America" boats, winning nine Harmsworth Trophies. The Harmsworth was the first international motor boat-racing trophy.

While famous athletes may be hard to meet, motorsports stars are often more accessible. The Midwest, where the sport continues to grow, may have prestigious races on the rivers and lakes, but the events have a casual and fan-friendly atmosphere.

The speed of racing and the thrill of competition bring people of all ages to the shores. Pilots line up their boats. Suddenly, a great roar fills the air. That roar keeps on for the whole race but by the end, there's a new roar—this time from the shore— as the fans scream for the winner.

aerodynamic: in boating, aerodynamic refers to the design or shape that allows a boat to move more quickly and easily on and through the water without resistance

buoys: the brightly colored floats that tell boats where to go during races

catamarans: boats that have two hulls

categories: the divisions of a group in different races; the racing categories are arranged by boat type and engine size

circuits (racing): the schedule or groups of planned races that take place over several months

displacement: the size of an engine that tells how powerful it is; the larger the displacement, the faster the boat

heat: in sporting competitions, a heat is one of several early, or preliminary, contests held to narrow down the field of competitors

horsepower: a unit to measure the power of engines

hull: the inside frame of a boat that can be made of plywood, fiberglass, or a combination of materials

hydroplane: a type of speedboat and also the (hydroplaning) action of the boat as it moves just above the surface of the water during a race

regions: parts of a country, or the world, divided by geographic areas

roostertail: the high splash, or wake, that a racing boat creates at the back of the boat, resembling a rooster's tail

shaft: the metal bar that connects an engine to a propeller

FURTHER READING

Books

Hydroplanes
Hans Hetrick
Chicago, IL
Edge Books
2010

Powerboat Racing
Jim Gigliotti
North Mankato, MN
Child's World
2012

Speedboat Racers
Michael Hauenstein
Berkeley Heights, NJ
Enslow Publishers
2010

Websites

The American Power Boat Association
www.apba.org/junior
The American Power Boat Association has
a special site with information and postings
for junior racers.

The Hydroplane and Raceboat Museum
www.thunderboats.ning.com
The Hydroplane and Raceboat Museum
has a great site with archives and photos
of racing boats.

The National Safe Boating Council
www.safeboatingcouncil.org/boating-
safety-sidekicks
The National Safe Boating Council has a
helpful site for adults, but also a kid-friendly
portion called Boating Safety Sidekicks with
puzzles and games.

RESOURCES

Organizations

American Power Boat Association
17640 East Nine Mile Road
Eastpointe, MI 48021
www.apba.org

Canadian Boating Federation
24 St-Louis, Suite 300
Valleyfield, QC Canada
J6T 1M4
www.cbfnc.ca

Page numbers in purple are images.

aerodynamic, 31
American Power
   Boat Association
   (APBA), 7, 8, 10,
   11, 26, 32, 37,
   38, 39

boat manufacturers,
   39
buoys, 5, 24, 40

catamarans, 10, 21,
   22, 23
circuit, 37, 38
cockpit, 32, 35, 40

displacement, 14
drag races, 24, 26,
   27, 38

F1 powerboats, 12

fiberglass, 24, 31
flat bottom, 10,
   13, 16

Gar Wood, 40, 41

heats, 19
helmets, 18, 33, 38
horsepower, 27
hull, 10, 13, 16,
   17, 21, 22, 24, 27
hydroplane, 10, 13,
   17, 18, 19, 21,
   29, 38
hydroplaning, 19, 29

inboard engines, 8

jet engines, 29,
   30, 32
junior racing classes,
   36, 37

INDEX

offshore, 6, 7, 11, **20**, **21**, **22**, 23, 24, 25
outboard engines, 8, **9**, 22

pilots, 31, 33, 34, 40, 41
profile, 32
propeller, 8, 16, 17

racecourses, 40
roostertail, 29
runabouts, 13, 14, **16**, 17, 38

shaft, 8

tail wings, 31
turbine engine, 30

unlimited hydroplane, **28**, 29, **31**, 32, **35**

V-boats, 22
V-hulls, 10, 21, 22

windshield, 33

About the Author

Collin MacArthur is a former automotive engineer with a master's degree in mechanical engineering. Today, Collin works as a freelance automotive interest writer. He lives in Florida with his wife, son, and dog.

48